JUPITER

The Giant of the Solar System

by Ellen Lawrence

Consultants:

Suzy Gazlay, MA
Recipient, Presidential Award for Excellence in Science Teaching

Kevin Yates
Fellow of the Royal Astronomical Society

Published in 2014 by Ruby Tuesday Books Ltd.

Editor: Mark J. Sachner
Designer: Emma Randall

Photo Credits:
NASA: Cover, 5 (top), 6, 8, 10, 11 (top), 12–13, 14–15,
16–17, 18–19, 20–21. Ruby Tuesday Books: 7, 22.
Shutterstock: 4–5, 9, 11 (bottom).

Library of Congress Control Number: 2013939982

ISBN 978-1-909673-12-0

Printed and published in the United States of America

For further information including rights and
permissions requests, please contact our Customer
Service Department at 877-337-8577.

Contents

Words shown in **bold** in the text are
explained in the glossary.

Welcome to Jupiter

Imagine flying to a world that is hundreds of millions of miles from Earth.

As your spacecraft gets close, you see colorful swirling clouds.

Inside the layer of clouds are strong winds and fierce storms that could destroy your spacecraft.

Even if you make it through the clouds, there is nowhere to land.

That's because this faraway world is a gigantic ball of **gases** and liquids.

Welcome to the **planet** Jupiter!

No humans have ever visited Jupiter, but spacecraft have. In 1972, a space **probe** called *Pioneer 10* was the first spacecraft to fly past the planet.

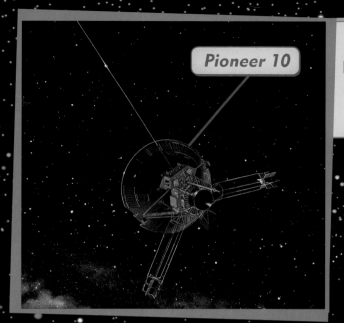

Pioneer 10

Pioneer 10 took hundreds of photos of Jupiter and beamed them back to Earth.

The clouds around Jupiter

The Solar System

Jupiter is moving through space at about 29,000 miles per hour (47,000 km/h).

It is moving in a huge circle around the Sun.

Jupiter is one of eight planets circling the Sun.

The planets are called Mercury, Venus, our home planet Earth, Mars, Jupiter, Saturn, Uranus, and Neptune.

Icy **comets** and large rocks, called **asteroids**, are also moving around the Sun.

Together, the Sun, the planets, and other space objects are called the **solar system**.

Most of the asteroids in the solar system are in a ring called the asteroid belt.

An asteroid

The Solar System
Jupiter is the fifth planet from the Sun.

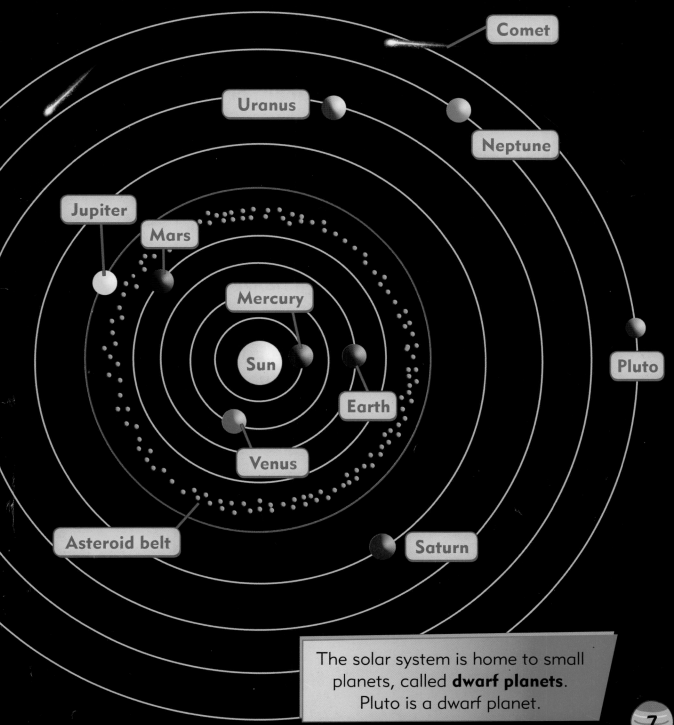

Comet

Uranus

Neptune

Jupiter

Mars

Mercury

Sun

Earth

Venus

Pluto

Asteroid belt

Saturn

The solar system is home to small planets, called **dwarf planets**. Pluto is a dwarf planet.

Jupiter's Amazing Journey

The time it takes a planet to **orbit**, or circle, the Sun once is called its year.

Earth takes just over 365 days to orbit the Sun, so a year on Earth lasts 365 days.

Jupiter is farther from the Sun than Earth, so it must make a much longer journey.

It takes Jupiter nearly 12 Earth years to orbit the Sun.

This means that a 12-year-old on Earth would just be turning 1 in Jupiter years!

As a planet orbits the Sun, it also spins, or **rotates**, like a top.

Jupiter

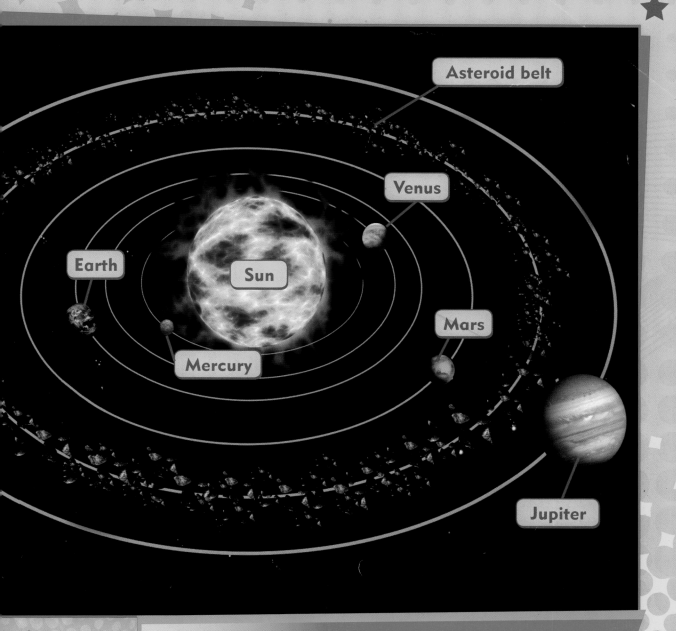

Asteroid belt

Venus

Earth

Sun

Mercury

Mars

Jupiter

To orbit the Sun once, Earth makes a journey of about 584 million miles (940 million km). Jupiter must make a journey of about 3 billion miles (5 billion km).

A Closer Look at Jupiter

Jupiter is by far the largest planet in the solar system.

It is **11** times as wide as Earth!

Unlike Earth, which is a rocky planet, Jupiter doesn't have a solid surface.

Jupiter has an **atmosphere** that is a thick layer of gases with an outer layer of clouds.

Beneath its atmosphere, the planet is a giant ball of liquids.

What Is Jupiter Made Of?

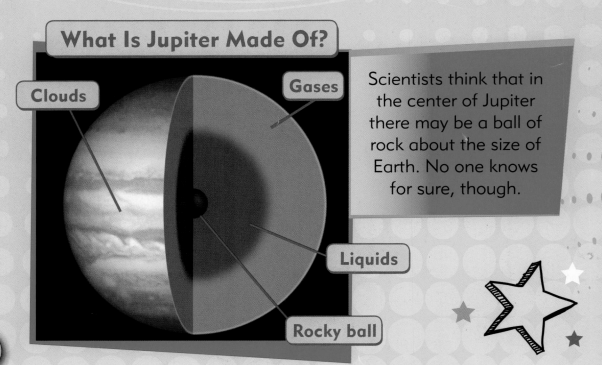

Clouds

Gases

Liquids

Rocky ball

Scientists think that in the center of Jupiter there may be a ball of rock about the size of Earth. No one knows for sure, though.

Jupiter

Earth

Our home planet Earth is a tiny world compared to giant Jupiter! It would be possible to fit 11 Earths across the face of Jupiter.

The Sun

Jupiter

Compared to the Sun, however, even gigantic Jupiter looks tiny!

The Great Red Spot

Jupiter is home to a huge storm called the Great Red Spot.

The Great Red Spot is like an enormous, spinning **hurricane**.

It is so big that it can easily be seen from Earth through a telescope.

In fact, people first saw the Great Red Spot when telescopes were invented 400 years ago.

This means the super-size hurricane has been going on for at least 400 years!

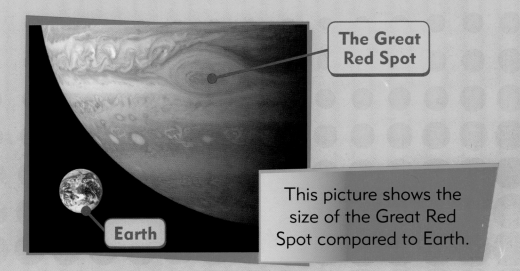

The Great Red Spot

Earth

This picture shows the size of the Great Red Spot compared to Earth.

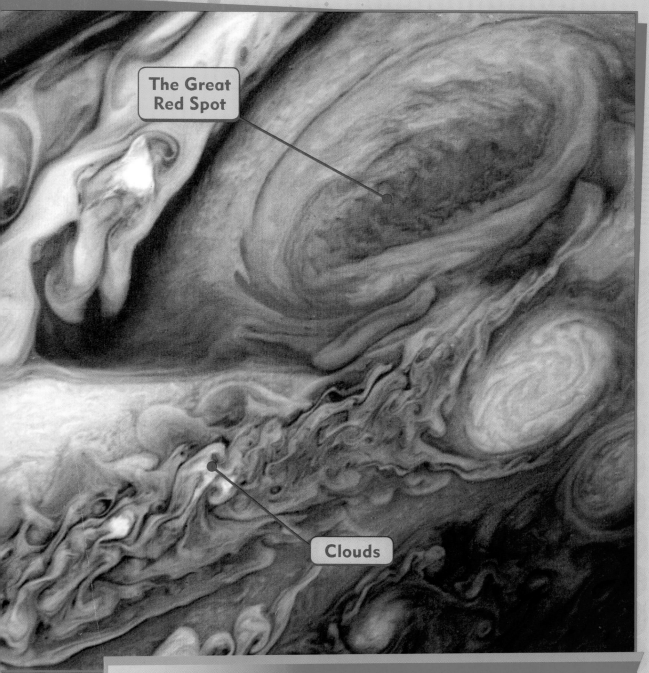

The Great Red Spot

Clouds

This picture was taken by a space probe called *Voyager 1*. It shows Jupiter's clouds and the Great Red Spot. The swirling, colorful patterns in the clouds are made by gases.

Jupiter's Family

Jupiter has an amazing family of smaller worlds circling it.

These rocky and icy space objects are the giant planet's **moons**.

Earth, our home planet, has just one moon.

Jupiter has at least 67 moons, and scientists are still discovering new ones!

Also circling Jupiter are four rings of dust and small pieces of rock.

Jupiter's Largest Moon

Mercury

Ganymede

Earth

Jupiter's largest moon is called Ganymede. It is the biggest moon in the whole solar system. It is even bigger than the planet Mercury.

Ganymede

Ganymede is covered with a layer of ice that may be 500 miles (800 km) thick!

Jupiter's Four Largest Moons

| Ganymede (GA-neh-mede) | Callisto (kuh-LIS-toh) | Io (EYE-oh) | Europa (yoo-ROH-puh) |

Amazing Moons

The spacecraft that visited Jupiter also discovered lots of information about the planet's moons.

The ground on one moon, Callisto, is covered with large holes called craters.

Jupiter's moon Io is home to more than 400 **volcanoes**.

The whole surface of Europa is covered with a deep ocean.

It is so cold on Europa, though, that the surface of the ocean is frozen!

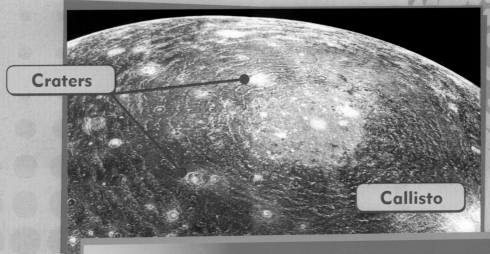

Craters

Callisto

The craters on Callisto were made by rocky objects, such as asteroids, that hit the moon.

Volcano

This picture shows one of the volcanoes on Io erupting.

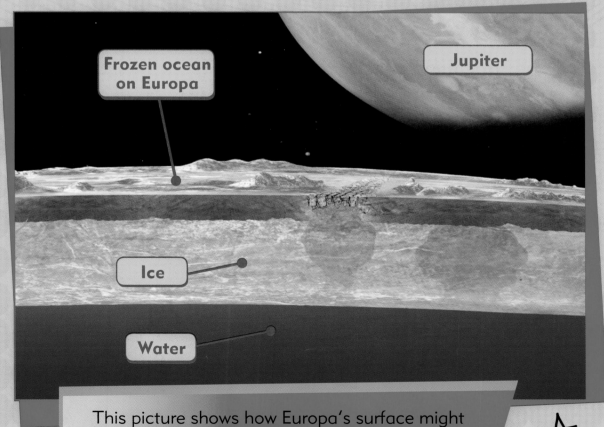

Frozen ocean on Europa

Jupiter

Ice

Water

This picture shows how Europa's surface might look. Scientists think that under the top layer of frozen ocean, there could be water.

Missions to Jupiter

In 1989, a space probe named *Galileo* (gal-uh-LAY-oh) left Earth on a mission to Jupiter.

Galileo orbited Jupiter for nearly eight years, studying the planet and its moons.

In August 2011, the newest Jupiter probe, *Juno,* was launched from Earth.

Juno will arrive at Jupiter in 2016.

Special equipment aboard *Juno* will let scientists see beneath Jupiter's clouds for the first time!

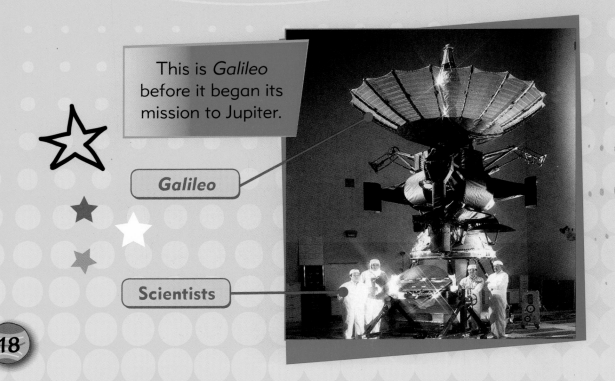

This is *Galileo* before it began its mission to Jupiter.

Galileo

Scientists

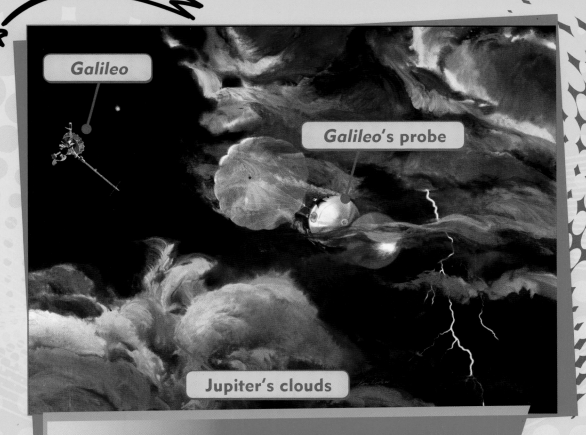

Galileo

Galileo's probe

Jupiter's clouds

This picture shows *Galileo* sending a smaller probe into Jupiter's clouds and atmosphere. The probe beamed information back to *Galileo* for 58 minutes.

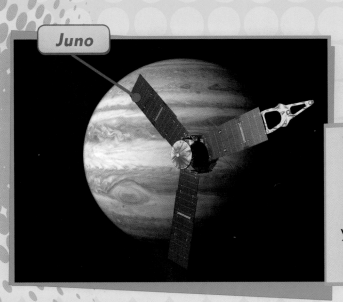

Juno

This picture shows how *Juno* will look when it reaches Jupiter. Its mission will last for one year, and it will orbit the planet 33 times.

Jupiter Fact File

Here are some key facts about Jupiter, the fifth planet from the Sun.

Discovery of Jupiter

Jupiter can be seen in the sky without a telescope. People have known it was there since ancient times.

How Jupiter got its name

The planet is named after the king of the Roman gods.

Planet sizes

This picture shows the sizes of the solar system's planets compared to each other.

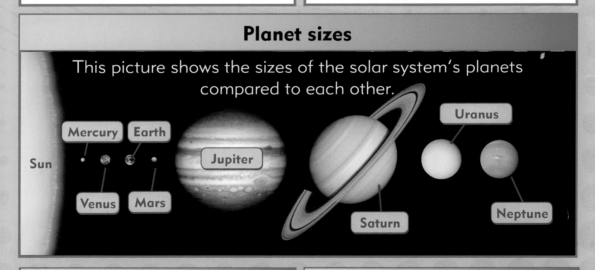

Sun · Mercury · Venus · Earth · Mars · Jupiter · Saturn · Uranus · Neptune

Jupiter's size

About 86,881 miles (139,822 km) across

How long it takes for Jupiter to rotate once

Nearly 10 Earth hours

Jupiter's distance from the Sun

The closest Jupiter gets to the Sun is 460,237,112 miles (740,679,835 km).

The farthest Jupiter gets from the Sun is 507,040,015 miles (816,001,807 km).

Average speed at which Jupiter orbits the Sun

29,205 miles per hour (47,002 km/h)

Jupiter's Moons

Jupiter has at least 67 moons. There are possibly more waiting to be discovered.

Length of Jupiter's orbit around the Sun

3,037,011,311 miles (4,887,595,931 km)

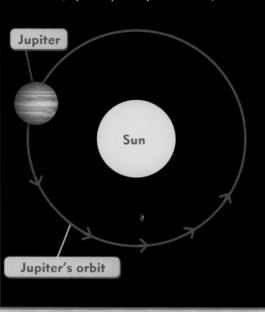

Jupiter

Sun

Jupiter's orbit

Length of a year on Jupiter

Nearly 4,333 Earth days (nearly 12 Earth years)

Temperature on Jupiter

-234°F (-148°C)

Get Crafty
Melted Wax Crayon Jupiter

Using melted wax crayons, make your own picture of Jupiter and its swirling, colorful clouds.

1. Cut two circles from the wax paper that are about the size of dinner plates.

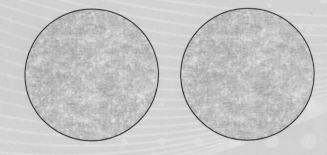

You will need:
- Wax paper
- Scissors
- Yellow, brown, and orange wax crayons
- A cheese grater
- An iron and an adult helper to use the iron

2. Grate the crayons onto one circle of wax paper. Be very careful not to rub your fingers against the grater.

3. Place the other piece of wax paper on top of the grated crayons to make a crayon sandwich.

4. Now ask an adult to iron your crayon sandwich using a cool iron. Keep ironing until the crayons melt and swirl together.

5. Hang your melted crayon Jupiter in a window to catch the Sun's light, or use it to make a space picture.

Glossary

asteroid (AS-teh-royd) A large rock that is orbiting the Sun. An asteroid can be as small as a car or bigger than a mountain.

atmosphere (AT-muh-sfeer) A layer of gases around a planet, moon, or star.

comet (KAH-mit) A space object made of ice, rock, and dust that is orbiting the Sun.

dwarf planet (DWARF PLAN-et) A round object in space that is orbiting the Sun. Dwarf planets are much smaller than the eight main planets.

gas (GASS) A substance, such as oxygen, that does not have a definite shape or size.

hurricane (HUR-uh-kane) A huge storm with powerful winds that circle around the center, or eye, of the storm. A hurricane can be hundreds of miles wide, and the winds can reach speeds of 200 miles per hour (320 km/h).

moon (MOON) An object in space that is orbiting a planet. Moons are usually made of rock, or rock and ice. Some are just a few miles wide. Others are hundreds of miles wide.

orbit (OR-bit) To circle, or move around, another object.

planet (PLAN-et) A large object in space that is orbiting the Sun. Some planets, such as Jupiter, are made of gases and liquids. Others, such as Earth, are made of rock.

probe (PROBE) A spacecraft that does not have any people aboard. Probes are controlled by scientists on Earth.

rotate (ROH-tate) To spin around.

solar system (SOH-ler SIS-tem) The Sun and all the objects that orbit it, such as planets, their moons, asteroids, and comets.

volcano (vol-KAY-noh) A mountain or hill that has an opening on it from which hot, liquid rock and gases erupt onto the surface of a planet or another body in space.

Index

Read More

Allyn, Daisy. *Jupiter: The Largest Planet (Our Solar System).* New York: Gareth Stevens (2011).

Hughes, Catherine D. *First Big Book of Space (National Geographic Little Kids).* Washington, D.C.: The National Geographic Society (2012).

Learn More Online

To learn more about Jupiter, go to
www.rubytuesdaybooks.com/jupiter